11·89

AL

S

OCT 15 1988

This Is a Let's-Read-and-Find-Out Science Book®

ANT CITIES

Written and illustrated by Arthur Dorros

THOMAS Y. CROWELL · NEW YORK

Other Recent Let's-Read-and-Find-Out Science Books® You Will Enjoy

Get Ready for Robots! · Gravity Is a Mystery · Journey into a Black Hole · Snow Is Falling
What Makes Day and Night · Turtle Talk · Bits and Bytes · The BASIC Book
Air Is All Around You · What the Moon Is Like · Sunshine Makes the Seasons · Hurricane Watch
What Happens to a Hamburger · My Visit to the Dinosaurs · Flash, Crash, Rumble, and Roll · Dinosaurs Are Different
Volcanoes · Germs Make Me Sick! · Meet the Computer · How to Talk to Your Computer
Rock Collecting · Is There Life in Outer Space? · Comets · All Kinds of Feet · Rain and Hail
Why I Cough, Sneeze, Shiver, Hiccup, & Yawn · You Can't Make a Move Without Your Muscles
The Sky Is Full of Stars · The Planets in Our Solar System · Digging Up Dinosaurs
No Measles, No Mumps for Me · When Birds Change Their Feathers · Birds Are Flying
A Jellyfish Is Not a Fish · Cactus in the Desert · Me and My Family Tree
Redwoods Are the Tallest Trees in the World · Shells Are Skeletons · Caves
Wild and Woolly Mammoths · The March of the Lemmings · Corals
Energy from the Sun · Corn Is Maize

The *Let's-Read-and-Find-Out Science Book* series was originated by Dr. Franklyn M. Branley, Astronomer Emeritus and former Chairman of The American Museum–Hayden Planetarium, and was formerly co-edited by him and Dr. Roma Gans, Professor Emeritus of Childhood Education, Teachers College, Columbia University. For a complete catalog of Let's-Read-and-Find-Out Science Books, write to Thomas Y. Crowell Junior Books, Harper & Row, Publishers, Inc., 10 East 53rd Street, New York, N.Y. 10022.

TO IRENE DORROS

Let's-Read-and-Find-Out Science Book is a registered trademark of Harper & Row, Publishers, Inc.

ANT CITIES
Copyright © 1987 by Arthur Dorros

Library of Congress Cataloging-in-Publication Data
Dorros, Arthur.
    Ant cities.

    (Let's-read-and-find-out science book)
    Summary: Explains how ants live and work together to build and maintain their cities.
    1. Ants—Nests—Juvenile literature. 2. Ants—Behavior—Juvenile literature. 3. Ants as pets—Juvenile literature. 4. Insects—Nests—Juvenile literature. 5. Insects—Behavior—Juvenile literature.
[1. Ants—Habits and behavior] I. Title. II. Series.
QL568.F7D75 1987   595.79′604524   85-48244
ISBN 0-690-04568-9
ISBN 0-690-04570-0 (lib. bdg.)

ANT CITIES

Have you seen ants busy running
over a hill of dirt?
They may look like they
are just running around.
But the ants built that hill to live in,
and each ant has work to do.

Some ants may disappear
into a small hole in the hill.
The hole is the door
to their nest.

These are harvester ants. Their nest is made of lots of rooms and tunnels. These little insects made them all.

When it is sunny, the top of the nest gets warm.

When it rains, water runs off the hill.

If it gets too wet near the top of the nest, the ants move below.

In winter the ants hibernate
in a deep room away from the cold.
They stay together in a ball
to keep warm.

Underneath the hill there
may be miles of tunnels and
hundreds of rooms.
The floors are worn smooth
by thousands of ant feet.
It is dark inside the nest.
But the ants stay cozy.

In the rooms of the nest, worker ants do many different kinds of work. It is like a city, a busy city of ants.

Some ants have brought in
food to the ant city. These
harvester ants like seeds.

A worker ant cracks
the husks off the seeds.
Another worker will
take the husks outside
to throw away.

The ants chew the seeds
to get the juices out.
Then they feed the juices
to the other ants.

Other workers store
seeds for the ants to eat
another time.

Not all ants store food.
But harvester ants do.

11

In one room of the nest, a queen ant lays eggs.
Workers carry the eggs away to other rooms to
take care of them.

Each ant city has to have at least one queen.
Without a queen there would be no ant city. All the
other ants in the ant city grow from the eggs the
queen lays.

At first the tiny eggs grow into larvae. The worker ants feed the larvae and lick them clean so they will grow well.

The larvae grow into pupae. The workers keep grooming the pupae until they grow into adults.

The queen ant lays thousands and thousands of eggs. Most of the eggs grow into worker ants. There may be only one queen ant in an ant city, but there can be many thousands of workers.

Queen

The queen is usually bigger than the other ants.
She lays eggs that grow into:

Workers

Workers are all females. They do the work in the ant city. They will also fight to protect the nest.

New Queens

New queens have wings. They use them to fly away to try to start new ant cities. Their wings drop off, and then the queens lay eggs.

Males

Males don't live in the nest for long. They fly away with the new queens to mate. Then they die.

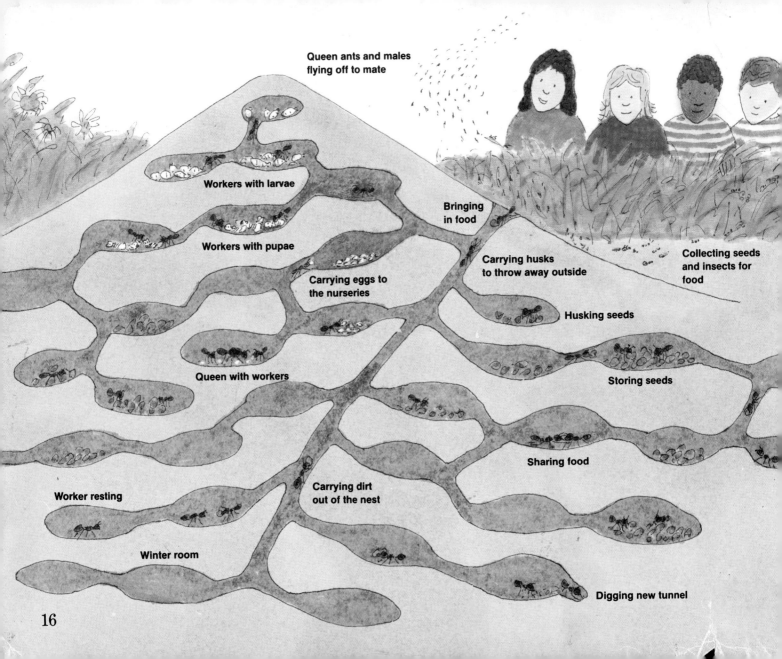

Queen ants and males
flying off to mate

Workers with larvae

Workers with pupae

Carrying eggs to
the nurseries

Bringing
in food

Carrying husks
to throw away outside

Collecting seeds
and insects for
food

Husking seeds

Queen with workers

Storing seeds

Sharing food

Worker resting

Carrying dirt
out of the nest

Winter room

Digging new tunnel

16

The queen doesn't tell the
workers what to do.
But the workers are busy.
Each ant has work to do.
Ants work together to keep
the whole ant city alive.

Workers make the nest bigger by digging new rooms and tunnels. They use their feet to dig like tiny dogs. Workers pick up pieces of dirt in their jaws and "beards" and carry them outside.

Harvester ants' hills can be
two feet high and six feet across.
Many other ants build smaller hills.

Dirt from the digging is what makes the anthill.
Ants are great diggers and builders. Imagine all the
tiny pieces of dirt it takes to build a hill two feet high.

Out around the harvester anthill, workers look for food. Harvester ants mostly eat seeds. But sometimes they eat insects, too.

Ants can bite and sting other insects to capture them or to protect themselves. Be careful, because some kinds of ants can bite or sting you, too. Harvester ants will bite or sting if you disturb their nest.

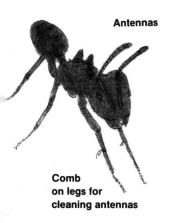

Antennas

Comb on legs for cleaning antennas

Ants use their antennas to help them find food. They touch and smell with their antennas.

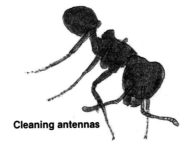

Cleaning antennas

Ants "talk" to each other by touching antennas.

If one ant finds food, others follow. Soon there will be a lot of ants carrying away lunch.

If one ant can't carry something, others may help. But each worker ant is strong. An ant can lift as much as fifty times its own weight. If people could lift like that, we could each lift a car.

The workers carry the food
back to the ant city.
Ants share the food they find.

Ants eat many foods.
But different kinds of ants
like different foods.
There are over 10,000
kinds of ants.

Formica ants mostly eat juices that they suck from insects they kill.

Cornfield ants like to eat the sweet juices, or "honeydew," they get from aphids. Aphids suck the juices from plants. Then the ants "milk" the aphids for honeydew.

Carpenter ants especially like sweet juices they can get from insects, and from plants, too.

Thief ants eat sweets and other food they find in people's houses and lying about.

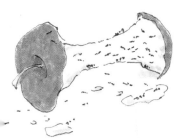

Leaf-cutting ants (parasol ants) make underground gardens with leaves they cut. They grow mushrooms in the gardens for food.

Army ants travel in large groups like armies. They devour huge numbers of insects, including termites.

The different kinds of ants have found many ways to make their cities, so they can live in many kinds of places.

Janitor ants make their nests in hollowed-out tree twigs. The soldier janitor ant—a kind of worker ant—has a big, plug-shaped head it can use for a door.

Doorway to janitor ants' nest

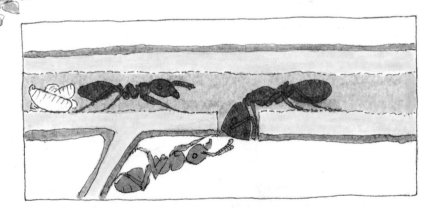

Many kinds of ants make hills or mounds. If you haven't seen harvester anthills, maybe you've seen the round-topped hills that formica ants make. Sometimes they cover their hills with thatch.

Formica ant

Pavement ants are tiny ants—⅛ inch long.
Harvester ants are about ¼ inch long.
Some ants are as big as 2 inches long.

Or you may have seen pavement ants.
They can live under the sidewalk.

Or carpenter ants, who build their nests
in rotting wood.

There are small ant cities with just a few ants.
There are big ant cities with many, many ants.
Ants have been found at the tops of the highest
buildings and on ships at sea.

Ants can make their cities almost anywhere.
Look around and you'll probably find an ant city,
busy with ants.

If you want to watch ants close up, try making a simple "ant farm." You can carefully collect ants yourself. If you want your farm to last a long time, be sure to include a queen.

Collecting jar

Remember when you collect any ants to be very careful. Some ants can bite or sting.

Fill to about here.

Lid of jar, with holes punched in it

- You can sift dirt into a jar, then put the ants in.
- Put a little bit of damp sponge into the jar so the ants have something to drink. If you put the water right into the jar, the ants might drown.
- Put a *little* food into the jar. Too much food, or the wrong food, will not be good for the ants. Remember, some ants like seeds, some like other insects. Some like sweets. Try to see what the ants are eating where you collect them.
- Now you have an "ant farm."
- Keep it in a dark place, so the ants will live the way they do underground. Take the jar into the light, and you can watch the ants.

Lid with holes

Sponge   Food

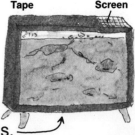

Dirt between two flat pieces of glass or plastic

Tape   Screen

Or you might want to make or buy an ant farm like this. ⟶